WHERE'S KIOSK KEITH?

Find Keith, critters and celebs, and relive
the most dramatic moments of every series!

Text by Mark Cowley
Illustrations by Bill Hope

hamlyn

Gino D'Acampo comes face to face with a particularly toothsome jungle snack in 2009.

In 2008, Joe Swash won the right to wear the coveted crown of twigs.

INTRODUCTION

Since it burst onto our screens way back in 2002, *I'm A Celebrity – Get Me Out Of Here!* has become one of the nation's favourite TV fixtures, the show that puts the star in starving, broadcast live from Australia each year over three unforgettable weeks.

For its legions of adoring fans, *I'm a Celebrity* has become a winter tradition, the curtain raiser for the festive season. Of course, in many ways, *I'm A Celebrity* is just like Christmas, except instead of turkey there's rice and beans, and instead of goodwill to all men, viewers make celebrities eat raw fish eyes. Makes you feel all Christmassy just thinking about it...

Over the years *I'm A Celebrity* has been showered with National Television Awards and BAFTAS; the format has been sold to countries such as France, Denmark, India, Sweden, Hungary, Holland, Romania and the USA – it's even one of the biggest shows on German TV. But what kind of sick, twisted mind first came up with the idea of dumping a load of terrified celebrities in the middle of the jungle, starving them and humiliating them with evil challenges before finally giving one of them a crown made of twigs?

Well, originally a group of TV producers decided to send a bunch of famous people on a jungle trek and film their adventure. That was the plan, but then someone came up with a revolutionary thought that would change telly forever: 'What if, instead of recording everything in advance and making a weekly series, we put out a show *every single night*? That way, viewers could see exactly what the celebs had been up to only a few hours ago.'

Of course, doing this back home in Britain would have been easy – there are plenty of studios where the action could be cut down into little packages very quickly. However, these celebrities were going to be stuck in the middle of the Australian rainforest.

Instead of telling the smart aleck producer where he could stick his idea, they placed the cast in a jungle camp so they couldn't move around too much. Then they built a massive TV production facility on the edge of the jungle, large enough for a crew of 600 people.

And finally, there was the masterstroke: asking two fresh-faced TV presenters from Newcastle to present the show, coming up with their own take on all the big stories live every night.

Before we knew it, the phrase 'Bushtucker Trial' had entered the English language, and Ant and Dec had discovered how funny it is to stand next to Uri Geller while he's trying to convince himself a beach worm is a piece of spaghetti.

An incredible 16 series later, *I'm A Celebrity – Get Me Out Of Here!* has gone from strength to strength, never losing its power to make us laugh, cry and occasionally retch. And to celebrate the show's enduring success, over the next 80 pages we're going to take you on your very own jungle adventure, a journey through the most memorable moments from all 16 series.

KIOSK KEITH: WHAT WE KNOW SO FAR

Little is known about Keith's early years, mainly because he was abandoned at birth and raised by a pack of wild dingoes, and dingoes are notoriously sloppy when it comes to record keeping.

Of course, being a human, living with dingoes was never going to be easy for Keith, and matters came to a head when he reached adulthood. After abandoning the pack, Keith went to school where he learned how to count on his fingers. Later on at college he added his thumbs, meaning Keith could finally get all the way up to ten. And with a topnotch Australian education in the bag, Keith pursued a lifetime ambition – to own his very own shop.

Keith's dream was to build a four-storey department store in the heart of Sydney, with his name proudly spelt out in towering golden letters over the entrance. But once Keith had spoken to the bank he opted for plan B – a small wooden shed in the middle of the jungle.

The Outback Shack threw open its doors and a legend was born.

Now it's over to you. Your job is to hunt down the great man himself in each picture, plus all 10 Bushtucker Trial stars and sundry animals, objects and celebrities, while taking a trip through some classic moments from *I'm A Celebrity – Get Me Out Of Here!*

Good luck and enjoy!

Ferne McCann screams her way through her first Bushtucker Trial in 2015.

HOW TO

Your mission is simple: to hunt down a man close to the hearts of all true *Celebrity* fans – Australia's favourite shopkeeper Kiosk Keith. Our mustachioed hero is hiding somewhere in every picture and it's down to you to spot him, as well as a variety of bugs, critters, celebrities and stars. It won't be easy, but with patience, application and a giant magnifying glass, you'll probably manage.

But before you get cracking, here's everything you need to know about Kiosk Keith.

Kiosk Keith in his natural environment – behind the counter of the Outback Shack.

2002

WINNER Tony Blackburn
RUNNER UP Tara Palmer-Tomkinson
3rd Christine Hamilton 4th Nell McAndrew
5th Rhona Cameron 6th Darren Day
7th Nigel Benn 8th Uri Geller

The first series of *I'm A Celebrity – Get Me Out Of Here!* was only 15 episodes long, but as it turned out that was plenty of time for the cast to leave their mark on television history. Veteran DJ Tony Blackburn became the first King of the Jungle, despite spending the entire two weeks obsessing about a pile of logs.

Tony Blackburn was still collecting logs on the last day, when socialite Tara Palmer-Tomkinson was packing to go home. But at least that was a peaceful pastime compared to what was going on in the rest of the camp.

Tara and actor Darren Day went through all the ups and downs of a relationship in the space of a fortnight. They shouted around the campfire. They tussled down at the creek. And in the end, they fell out over a fart.

But while Tara and Darren had a love-hate relationship, it was more hate-hate for Nigel Benn. The Dark Destroyer had taken on Chris Eubank and survived. But nothing could have prepared him for the most terrifying opponent he'd ever come up against – Scottish comedian Rhona Cameron. The first fight they had was over chicken breasts, and things just escalated from there. Their arguments took in sexuality and religion, and ended up with Nigel wishing Rhona was a bloke so he could knock her sparko.

In the midst of the madness, Rhona made a speech Churchill himself would have been proud of... if he'd been stuck in the jungle with a load of crazy celebrities.

Nell McAndrew reaches for the stars in the Bucking Bronco trial.

Christine Hamilton tries to get to grips with some piglets during Pig Chase.

Rhona Cameron makes her impassioned speech to the camp.

Nigel Benn puts his hand into the snake pit in the second trial.

KEY MOMENTS

Tony's love affair with the wood pile ❦ Rhona and Nigel's fraught exchanges ❦ Uri's Bushtucker Bonanza trial ❦ Tara and Darren's whirlwind romance ❦ Nell's Bucking Bronco ❦ Christine chasing a pig ❦ Nigel being bitten by a snake ❦ Uri being the first to leave

LIST OF TRIALS

1	Bug Shower	Tara	8/8 stars
2	Snake Surprise	Nigel	5/8 stars
3	Buried Alive	Rhona	6/8 stars
4	Bushtucker Bonanza	Uri	8/8 stars
5	Pig Chase	Christine	7/7 stars
6	Hell Holes	Darren	8/8 stars
7	Night Watch	Nigel	8/8 stars

8	Stinking Swamp	Darren	7/7 stars
9	Sneaky Snake Run	Tony	2/6 stars
10	Bucking Bronco	Nell	5/5 stars
11	Spider Web	Tony	3/4 stars
12	Underwater Treasure Hunt	Christine	2/3 stars
13	Final Trial	Tara and Tony	8/8 stars

WHAT TO FIND

Can you spot Keith, the stars, three images from the cut scenes – a chameleon's eye, a bat and a machete – and our worthy winner, Tony?

Chameleon's eye

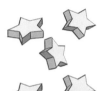

10 stars

Keith

Tony

Fruit bat

Machete in tree

5

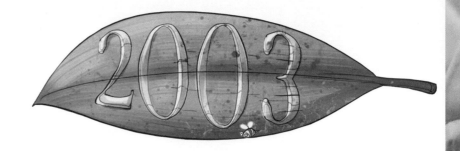

WINNER Phil Tufnell

RUNNER UP John Fashanu

3rd Linda Barker 4th Wayne Sleep
5th Antony Worrall Thompson
6th Toyah Wilcox 7th Catalina Guirado
8th Chris Bisson 9th Danniella Westbrook
10th Siân Lloyd

Antony Worrall Thompson addresses his camp mates during the Great Sausage Rebellion.

Wayne Sleep dons a waffle balaclava during the Rat Food Suit trial.

Series 2 of *I'm A Celebrity – Get Me Out Of Here!* was just about the most bad tempered of the lot.

The celebrities weren't always arguing with each other, they were also having a right old go at the producers. As ever, the anger stemmed from food, or the lack of it, and matters came to a head on the 'night of the short sausages'. Chef Antony Worrall Thompson led a delegation of furious celebs out of the camp and over the bridge, where they threatened to quit the show unless they were given more bangers for their dinner.

Eventually things calmed down and the rebels returned to camp, while some terrified producers headed off home for a cry.

When they weren't arguing with the producers, the celebs were up to plenty of other mischief. Dancer Wayne Sleep jumped clean through his bed and nearly broke his leg, while former footballer John Fashanu discovered he had a fear of pretty much everything – including crossing the bridge to take on a Bushtucker Trial.

It was in Series 2 that we learned just how mean viewers can be, ruthlessly sending celebrities to take on endless trials if they so much as show a whiff of fear.

Before too long Danniella Westbrook found the whole thing too stressful and, missing her kids, she jumped ship and headed back to her hotel.

Ultimately it was cricket legend and all-round geezer Phil Tufnell whom viewers decided had earned the right to be crowned King of the Jungle.

WHAT TO FIND

You need to find a discarded mobile phone, a sausage with a fork stuck in it, a stick insect enjoying a cup of tea and, of course, the stars and Keith.

Mobile phone

10 stars

Keith

Sausage with a fork in it

Stick insect with a cuppa

KEY MOMENTS

Antony leading a protest for more sausages ▮ Wayne nearly breaking his leg ▮ John being scared of the bridge ▮ Danniella walking out ▮ John filling his trousers full of insects ▮ Wayne being attacked by rats with waffles strapped to him ▮ Phil being crowned King of the Jungle

LIST OF TRIALS

1	Keep It In Your Pants	John	7/10 stars
2	Croc Pit	Catalina	10/10 stars
3	Rat Food Suit	Wayne	2/10 stars
4	Bridge of Doom	John	8/10 stars
5	Catch a Falling Star	Danniella	3/10 stars
6	Snake Pit	John	4/10 stars
7	Bobbing for Stars	John	9/10 stars
8	What Lies Within	Antony	5/10 stars
9	Shooting Stars	Phil	8/9 stars

10	Teatime in Hell	Toyah	5/8 stars
11	Terror in the Trees	Linda	7/7 stars
12	Jungle Slide	Phil	4/6 stars
13	Wheel of Horror	Linda	5/5 stars
14	Eel Helmet	John	4/4 stars
15	Balance: Bushtucker Bonanza	Phil	5/5 stars
16	Determination: Eel Transfer	Linda	4/5 stars
17	Reach: Log Bog	John	5/5 stars

JAN/FEB 2004

WINNER Kerry Katona

RUNNER UP Jennie Bond

3rd Peter Andre 4th Lord Brocket 5th Katie Price
6th Alex Best 7th John Lydon 8th Neil 'Razor' Ruddock 9th Diane Modahl
10th Mike Read

The third series of *I'm A Celebrity – Get Me Out Of Here!* was a bona fide classic with a wealth of standout moments.

At the heart of it all was the thrilling romance between singer Peter Andre and Katie Price (previously known as Jordan), a romance that actually ended in the pair of them walking down the aisle.

And as well as falling in love, Peter also found the time to write his classic hit *Insania* about life in the jungle.

Not everybody loved Jordan as much as Peter, and punk rocker John Lydon for one couldn't stand the sight of the model. In the end John stormed off the show, so we'll never know how far he could have gone.

Ultimately Kerry Katona became the first-ever Queen of the Jungle. On her arrival in camp, it looked like the Atomic Kitten singer wasn't going to last a day, but she went on what telly people love to call a 'journey' and by the end of two weeks she'd conquered her fears and won the nation's hearts in the process.

To win her crown, Kerry had to overcome Peter Andre and former royal reporter Jennie Bond, who put on a fantastic stiff-upper-lip performance in a last Bushtucker Trial, munching on yabbies, leaf mimics, stick insects and more without batting an eyelid.

It was a magnificent performance and a fitting ending to one of the best series of the lot.

Peter Andre's *Insania* gets its first airing. The song went on to reach No. 3 in the UK charts.

Jennie Bond and Peter Andre successfully balance out the Celebrity See–saw and bag a maximum six stars.

Jennie Bond takes on the final trial in Bushtucker Bonanza.

A 'tarred and feathered' Alex Best.

KEY MOMENTS

Katie and Peter's romance ❧ Peter writing *Insania* ❧ John storming off the show ❧ Peter and Jennie riding a see-saw ❧ John facing 12 hungry ostriches ❧ Jennie putting in a great performance on the final Bushtucker Trial ❧ Kerry winning

WHAT TO FIND

Aside from Keith and the stars, can you find a feathered Alex, a bespectacled ostrich, a camp mess tin and an indigenous scorpion?

Feathered Alex

10 stars

Scorpion wearing a hat

Keith

An ostrich in shades

Mess tin

LIST OF TRIALS

1	Fill Your Face	Katie and Neil	10/10 stars
2	Beat the Birds	John	6/10 stars
3	Jungle Houdini	Kerry	2/10 stars
4	Use Your Head	Peter	10/10 stars
5	Danger Down Under	Jennie	10/10 stars
6	Ladder Lottery	Lord Brocket	6/10 stars
7	Bite to Bite	Katie and Kerry	7/10 stars
8	Tunnel of Terror	Alex	7/10 stars
9	Row for Your Life	Diane and Peter	0/9 stars
10	Splash and Grab	Katie	3/8 stars
11	Torture Tank	Lord Brocket	7/7 stars
12	Celebrity See-saw	Jennie and Peter	6/6 stars
13	Snake Lake	Katie	3/5 stars
14	Hell Hill	Jennie, Kerry, Lord Brocket and Peter	2/4 stars
15	Cockroach Attack	Kerry	0/5 stars
16	Spider Man	Peter	5/5 stars
17	Bushtucker Bonanza	Jennie	5/5 stars

WINNER Joe Pasquale

RUNNER UP Paul Burrell

3rd Fran Cosgrave 4th Janet Street-Porter
5th Sophie Anderton 6th Antonio Fargas
7th Sheila Ferguson 8th Vic Reeves
9th Nancy Sorrell 10th Natalie Appleton
11th Brian Harvey

Brian Harvey takes on the fateful House of Pies.

Natalie Appleton goes shopping in the treetops in her Canopy Calamity trial.

Series 4 of *I'm A Celebrity* was a particularly crazy couple of weeks in the jungle.

Former East 17 singer Brian Harvey set the tone for the series when he had a big falling out with Janet Street-Porter over his non-stop farting. Which wasn't really his fault, considering the amount of beans everyone has to eat in the jungle.

Poor old Brian finally flipped after taking on the hideous Bushtucker Trial, House of Pies. After being trapped in a box with a million flies, Brian was never really the same again, and left the show early, presumably to go and buy a can of insect repellent. Janet didn't reserve her fury for Brian though. On one memorable occasion when she'd gone for a walk, she turned on a cameraman, giving him the fright of his life.

One person who would never take a stroll in the jungle voluntarily was ex-All Saints singer, Natalie Appleton. Natalie was literally terrified of everything. On her way into the jungle she screamed and uttered a line that has haunted her ever since, 'Oooooh – I touched a tree!'

But no one is better remembered for Series 4 than the former butler to Diana Princess of Wales, Paul Burrell. Paul was chosen to face the Hell Holes in his Bushtucker Trial, and his screeching, grimacing and swivel-eyed terror instantly became one of the most memorable moments in *I'm A Celebrity* history.

On a calmer note, Joe Pasquale spent his entire time in the jungle befriending a pair of emus he named Ant and Dec. Partly it was because he loved them. Partly it was to stay the hell away from Natalie Appleton and model Sophie Anderton, who'd been at each other's throats since the moment they arrived in camp.

Sophie Anderton enters the jungle on horseback.

Laughing his way through the series, Joe Pasquale in a pit of rats.

Viewers loved Joe's good-natured silliness and it was no surprise when he was crowned King.

KEY MOMENTS

Five celebrities riding into camp on horseback ❦ Joe in a pit of rats in Danger Down Under ❦ Brian storming out ❦ Joe being the first celebrity to win all of the stars in Hell-o-copter ❦ Janet scaring a cameraman ❦ Joe befriending two emus ❦ Paul screeching in Hell Holes ❦ Joe winning

LIST OF TRIALS

1	Stake Out	Antonio, Fran and Joe	4/10 stars
2	Canopy Calamity	Natalie	7/10 stars
3	Snake Strike	Janet	9/10 stars
4	House of Pies	Brian	2/10 stars
5	Temple of Doom	Paul	6/11 stars
6	Leap of Faith	Natalie	2/11 stars
7	Snap	Natalie and Sophie	5/10 stars
8	Slither River	Natalie	1/10 stars
9	On Your Knees	Sheila	6/9 stars

10	Hell-o-copter	Joe	8/8 stars
11	Fill Your Face	Antonio	4/7 stars
12	Slither River 2	Fran	3/6 stars
13	Hump It!	Janet and Sophie	3/5 stars
14	Hell Holes	Paul	5/5 stars
15	Hell Hill 2	Fran, Janet, Joe and Paul	3/4 stars
16	Eel Helmet	Fran	5/5 stars
17	Bushtucker Bonanza	Paul	5/5 stars
18	Danger Down Under	Joe	5/5 stars

WHAT TO FIND

Can you spot Antonio in riding gear, a camel in sunglasses, those loveable baby emus and our winner, Joe, as well as Keith and all the stars?

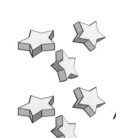

Antonio wearing a riding hat

10 stars

Keith

Joe as King of the Jungle

Two baby emus

Camel in sunglasses

Series 5 of I'm A Celebrity – Get Me Out Of Here! was easily the friendliest we had ever seen. There was no arguing, no fighting, just loads of sunny smiles and mutual admiration. And people absolutely loved it. Because bickering or not, there were plenty of classic moments along the way.

During her time in camp former *Emmerdale* star Sheree Murphy conquered just about every fear in the book. She spent a terrifying night in the Jungle Jail, and that was after she'd jumped out of a helicopter. And as if that wasn't enough, poor old Sheree also found herself taking on the terrors of an eating trial on her final day in the jungle. She fully deserved her runner-up position.

Then there was the golden moment when little Jimmy Osmond came face to face with a load of scary-looking kangaroos in his Bushtucker Trial. The kangaroos prompted Ant and Dec to come up with one of the best jokes of the series: 'A group of terrifying creatures with wild staring eyes and huge teeth, the Osmonds had a string of hits in the early '70s.'

The weirdest Bushtucker Trial of the series saw comedy double act Tommy Cannon and Bobby Ball suspended on a high wire for Fright of the Bumblebees, dressed in hilarious bee costumes and milking their moment for all it was worth. Sadly Tommy got his marching orders soon after, leaving Bobby to fly the flag on his own.

One of the highlights of Series 5 was the unlikely friendship David 'The Duke' Dickinson struck up with *EastEnders* star Sid Owen. Their odd-couple bromance hit its peak as the two of them headed off to take on a Celebrity Chest Challenge together. Sid was attached to

Cannon and Ball back on prime time TV with Fright of the Bumblebees.

The nation's favourite, Carol Thatcher, takes on Highway to Hell.

a giant elastic wire and David stood beneath him shrieking 'Get down Sid!' at the top of his lungs.

Carol Thatcher, the daughter of former Prine Minister Margaret Thatcher, won over the public with her never-say-die attitude as she faced endless challenges, from steering a buggy over an abyss to tackling her very own eating trial.

Carol was also involved in one of the greatest moments in *I'm A Celebrity* history. She got herself in a spot of hot water when she was caught on camera taking a wee in camp at night. Producers always tell the celebrities not to do this because it attracts snakes. The wee-gate saga rumbled on for days, while Carol refused to confess to the crime.

That didn't prevent Carol from being crowned the Queen of the Jungle. We never found out what her mum made of that.

Singing for his dinner, Antony Costa does Scaryoke.

KEY MOMENTS

Tommy and Bobby in Fright of the Bumble Bees ❦ David and Sid's bromance ❦ Carol and wee-gate ❦ Antony doing Scaryoke ❦ Carol driving a cart in Highway to Hell ❦ Ant and Dec Farm ❦ Carol being crowned Queen of the Jungle

LIST OF TRIALS

#	Trial	Contestant	Stars
1	Scales of Jungle Justice	David and Sid	4/10 stars
2	Highway to Hell	Carol	4/9 stars
3	Kangaroo Court	Jimmy	4/9 stars
4	Ant and Dec Farm	Kimberley	4/9 stars
5	Bush Tucker Bluff	Carol and Jilly	8/9 stars
6	Rocky Horror	Sheree	5/11 stars
7	Fright of the Bumblebees	Bobby and Tommy	9/11 stars
8	Scaryoke	Antony	4/11 stars
9	Dreadful Drop	Kimberley and Sheree	7/12 stars
10	Panic Station	Jenny	9/9 stars
11	Jungle Strike	Antony, Bobby and Sid	2/9 stars
12	Lily Lottery	Jimmy	4/7 stars
13	Ant and Dec Farm 2	Sid	4/7 stars
14	Noah's Ark	Carol	5/5 stars
15	Satan's Slope	Carol, Jimmy, Sheree and Sid	4/4 stars
16	Snake Strike	Carol	5/5 stars
17	Bushtucker Bonanza	Sid	3/5 stars
18	Danger Down Under	Sheree	5/5 stars

WHAT TO FIND

Can you locate the 'frightening' bee, Tommy Cannon, a cockatoo piñata, some stinky fish eyes, the baby emus, the stars and Keith?

Trial bee

Keith

Piñata

Fish eyes

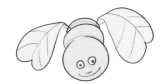
10 stars

Cannon (without Ball)

Two baby emus

WINNER Matt Willis

RUNNER UP Myleene Klass

3rd Jason Donovan 4th David Gest
5th Dean Gaffney 6th Jan Leeming
7th Malandra Burrows 8th Phina Oruche
9th Lauren Booth 10th Faith Brown
11th Scott Henshall 12th Toby Anstis

Mylene Klass and Malandra Burrows teeter among the treetops in the Skyscrape trial.

Myleene Klass takes a shower in her unforgettable white bikini.

For a lot of viewers, the most memorable moment of *I'm A Celebrity – Get Me Out Of Here!* Series 6 has to be that legendary Celebrity Chest Challenge, when the key to the chest was hidden in a bar of soap and singer and presenter Myleene Klass had to take a bath to release it. That, and regular showers in the now-infamous white bikini, made dads across the nation very grateful.

This series also introduced one of the great *I'm A Celebrity* eccentrics, music producer and best friend of Michael Jackson, the late, great David Gest. David loved life in the jungle, mainly because there were cameras pointed at him all the time. He absolutely adored the attention.

David's tall tales had the rest of the camp in stitches, such as the one he told Myleene in which he was born in Taiwan, his dad was a fisherman and his mother was a nun. Oh, and that both of his parents only had the one leg. Myleene fell for it hook, line and sinker. David Gest – a jungle legend.

Then there was David's right-hand man, Jason Donovan. The former *Neighbours* star and singer kept the viewers at home in stitches as we watched him happily go bonkers in the jungle. Disgusting trials, horrible challenges and more, whatever was thrown at Jason he met with a smile, and it was no surprise to see him make it all the way to the final day of the series.

But if we thought Jason Donovan was going a bit loopy, nothing could have prepared us for the late arrival of *EastEnders* star Dean Gaffney and what was, quite simply, the greatest live Bushtucker Trial of them all. As Dean made his way through the terrors of the Jungle Spa, the entire nation was falling on the floor with laughter. Dean retched, heaved, gagged, threw up, screamed and wailed and at one point very possibly cried. It was a trial you can watch again and again. And if you don't believe me, try and track it down – it never fails to put a smile on your face.

All these antics aside, in Series 6 there was only going to be one winner and that was boy band heart throb Matt Willis. The Busted guitarist quietly charmed his way to the final and claimed the ultimate prize of his very own jungle crown.

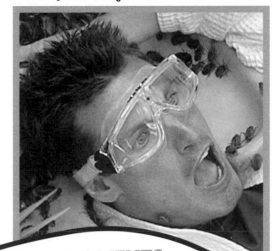

Dean Gaffney suffers through the funniest Bushtucker Trial ever.

KEY MOMENTS

Myleene taking a bath for the Celebrity Chest Challenge ❦ David's entertaining stories ❦ Dean's live Bushtucker Trial ❦ The see-saw, treetop Skyscrape trial ❦ Jan facing llamas, ostriches and even a bull in Bull in a China Shop ❦ Jan and Scott parachuting on to the beach in a head-to-head trial ❦ Matt winning

LIST OF TRIALS

1	Mineshaft Misery	Jan and Toby	2/10 stars
2	Flash Flood	David	6/10 stars
3	Jungle Boogie	Scott	1/10 stars
4	Treetop Terror	Jan and Scott	4/10 stars
5	Jungle Spa	Dean	9/11 stars
6	Operation	Phina and Jason	6/12 stars
7	Snake Bite	Jan	10/12 stars
8	Bull in a China Shop	Jan	6/12 stars
9	Catch a Falling Star	Jan and Scott	Jan wins
10	Bushtucker Duel	Jan and Scott	Scott wins
11	What Lurks Beneath	Phina and Scott	Phina wins
12	Thunderball	Jason, Malandra and Matt	3/11 stars

13	Jungle Falls	Dean, Lauren and Phina	6/10 stars
14	Tomb of Torment	Myleene	9/9 stars
15	Shooting Gallery	David, Jason and Matt	1/8 stars
16	Skyscrape	Malandra and Myleene	5/7 stars
17	Temple of Doom	Dean	5/6 stars
18	Celebrity Cyclone	Jason, Myleene and Matt	5/5 stars
19	Bushtucker Bonanza	Matt	5/5 stars
20	Fill Your Face	Jason	5/5 stars
21	Scaryoke	Myleene	5/5 stars

WHAT TO FIND

Aside from Keith and the stars, can you spot Dean in the Jungle Spa, Jan wearing the bottom half of a wallaby suit, a yabbie and a cool llama?

Yabbie

Keith

10 stars

Dean in the critter hairdryer

Llama in shades

Jan with half a wallaby costume

25

WINNER
Christopher Biggins
RUNNER UP Janice Dickinson

3rd Jason 'J' Brown 4th Cerys Matthews 5th Gemma Atkinson
6th Anna Ryder Richardson 7th Rodney Marsh
8th John Burton-Race 9th Lynne Franks
10th Katie Hopkins
11th Marc Bannerman

Series 7 of I'm A Celebrity – Get Me Out Of Here! turned out to be an absolute belter. Maybe there was something in the water, but the cast that year were completely bonkers from the moment they arrived in the Australian rainforest.

At the centre of it all was American supermodel Janice Dickinson. Janice had what is best described as a bit of a potty mouth. And when Janice decided that she didn't like someone, she was more than happy to aim that mouth of hers and let fly.

This was bad news for earth mother and PR guru Lynne Franks, or 'you shrew', as Janice famously addressed her. The two ladies insulted each other for pretty much their entire two weeks together in the jungle.

Not to be left out, TV chef John Burton-Race and former footballer Rodney Marsh had their own ding dongs around the campfire with Lynne, who, for someone who had spent decades working in the PR industry, seemed to find it surprisingly difficult to maintain good public relations with anyone.

But just when we thought the whole series might turn into one vast endless argument about how to boil a crocodile's foot, in came late arrival to the camp Christopher Biggins. Funny, saucy and able to laugh through some very unpleasant Bushtucker Trials, Biggins put a smile on the nation's faces from the moment he made his larger-than-life entrance.

Series 7 also witnessed that rarest of jungle events, a genuine, bona fide romance between two campers. Catatonia singer and radio DJ Cerys Matthews made headlines when she enjoyed a whirlwind romance with

Lynne Franks expresses her opinion in another 'frank discussion'.

In the Web Sight trial, Christopher Biggins only has eyes for the stars.

Biggins: from national treasure to King of the Jungle.

former *Eastenders* actor Marc Bannerman, although the viewing public put paid to the budding relationship pretty quickly by booting him out of the jungle first.

In the end, however, there could only ever be one King of the Jungle this year, and that was the man, the myth, the legend himself – Biggins.

KEY MOMENTS

Lynne and Janice's raging feud ❧ Biggins's late entry ❧ Cerys and Marc's jungle romance ❧ Biggins winning all seven stars in Web Sight ❧ Jason 'J' and John in Dreadful Drop ❧ Cerys swinging through the jungle in Dam Vines ❧ Jason 'J' getting stuck in a bubble of creatures in Tabletop Terror ❧ Biggins winning

LIST OF TRIALS

#	Trial	Contestants	Result
1	Wheel of Misfortune	Marc and Janice	Marc wins
2	Rumble Rally	Rodney and Janice	Janice wins
3	Sushi Train of Pain	John and Janice	John wins
4	In Grave Danger	Katie	10/10 stars
5	Jungle Jeopardy	Biggins and Janice	7/11 stars
6	Nip/Pluck	Janice and Lynn	7/11 stars
7	Catch a Crawling Star	Janice and Rodney	2/11 stars
8	The Tunnel of Terror	Lynne	5/11 stars
9	Uneasy Rider	Jason 'J' and Janice	10/11 stars
10	Jungle Sweetshop	Janice and Lynne	9/11 stars
11	Bat Out of Hell	Cerys and Gemma	6/10 stars
12	Dreaded Water	Anna and Rodney	9/9 stars
13	Dreadful Drop	Jason 'J' and John	6/8 stars
14	Web Sight	Biggins	7/7 stars
15	The Terror Train & The Temple of Doom	Jason 'J' and Gemma	4/6 stars
16	Dam Vines	Cerys	2/5 stars
17	Tabletop Terror	Jason 'J'	5/5 stars
18	Celebrity Cyclone	Cerys, Biggins, Jason 'J' and Janice	3/4 stars
19	Stakeout	Janice	5/5 stars
20	Bushtucker Bonanza	Biggins	5/5 stars
21	Flash Flood	Jason 'J'	4/5 stars

WHAT TO FIND

Can you find Jason 'J' in a koala costume and the other stars of the jungle panto, as well as Keith and all the stars?

Panto dame

Keith

Goldilocks

Jason 'J' as a koala

10 stars

The good fairy

Tunnel of Terror

2008

Series 8 of *I'm A Celebrity – Get Me Out Of Here!* will probably be remembered above all for one of the most genuinely touching friendships ever to emerge in the jungle.

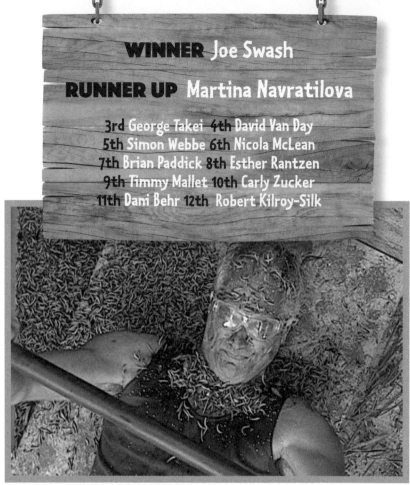

WINNER Joe Swash

RUNNER UP Martina Navratilova

3rd George Takei 4th David Van Day
5th Simon Webbe 6th Nicola McLean
7th Brian Paddick 8th Esther Rantzen
9th Timmy Mallet 10th Carly Zucker
11th Dani Behr 12th Robert Kilroy-Silk

Covered in bugs and critters, Robert Kilroy-Silk works out in the Jungle Gym.

From the second they laid eyes on each other, former *EastEnders* star Joe Swash and *Star Trek* legend George Takei, AKA Sulu, clicked. And millions of viewers had the pleasure of watching a cross-generational, transatlantic bromance like no other develop in camp. George absolutely adored Joe, and the feeling was entirely mutual. Their relationship was perfectly captured in the moment Joe taught George to sing a very rude song called *Olli Olli Olli* – which are also about the only three words in the song that are fit to print!

But don't go thinking that the eighth series was a complete love-in. Oh no. Because two men had very different plans in mind. Late arrivals to the camp David Van Day from '80s group Dollar and children's TV presenter Timmy Mallet managed to turn that place upside down from the day they walked in.

David was lazy, rude and gleefully childish. He wound up every other person in the jungle, although model Nicola McLean was the camper whose nose he definitely got up most. The singer hissed, booed and generally did everything in his power to rile Nicola, while national treasure Esther Rantzen desperately attempted to be the voice of reason.

David and Timmy's bad behaviour came to a head when TV presenter and former politician Robert Kilroy-Silk was taking part in a live Bushtucker Trial. The duo heckled him throughout, infuriating Kilroy-Silk, which was very, very naughty. And very, very funny.

In a mischievous twist, the producers at one point sent David and Nicola off alone together to the Jungle Car Wash for their very own challenge, a day she'll no doubt remember fondly for the rest of her life.

When they weren't busy winding everyone up, David and Timmy actually wrote a song together – the truly awful *Biff Baff Boff (We're Celebrities)*, a ditty that made Peter Andre's *Insania* sound like Beethoven's Fifth Symphony in comparison.

Timmy's time in the jungle came to an end in a jaw-dropping visit to the Last Chance Saloon. Taking on retired policeman Brian Paddick, Timmy had to drink a series of truly disgusting cocktails. Despite his best efforts he was pipped at the post and had to say his goodbyes.

With all this going on it's easy to forget that this series featured a genuine tennis legend. Martina Navratilova was a real trouper, and showed that she hadn't lost her athletic ability in her first trial, Car-nage, which saw her leaping over a row of suspended Mini cars.

This was one of those series where you just knew who was ultimately going to come out on top: Joe Swash's name was written on the jungle crown from day one. And it's fitting that such a great winner has been part of the programme all the way up to the present, with his presenting role on ITV2's spin-off show, *I'm A Celebrity – Get Me Out Of Here NOW!*, later known as *I'm A Celebrity: Extra Camp*.

Great cast. Great series.

Nicola McLean earns treats for the camp at the Jungle Car Wash.

KEY MOMENTS

Yellow team contestants entering camp on floating feet ❧ David and Timmy getting caught in the Mantrap ❧ George and Joe's blossoming friendship ❧ David and Timmy laughing at Robert in Jungle Gym ❧ Martina showing off her athletic ability in Car-nage ❧ Timmy and Brian drinking horrible concoctions in Last Chance Saloon ❧ Joe being crowned King of the Jungle

LIST OF TRIALS

1	Long Drop	Dani and Carly	Dani wins
2	I Scream Van	Joe and Nicola	Nicola wins
3	Chambers of Horror	Joe and Robert	Joe wins
4	John Travolting	Robert	10/10 stars
5	Jungle Gym	Robert	12/12 stars
6	Holey Moley	David	5/12 stars
7	Critter Chaos	Timmy	12/12 stars
8	Cavern of Calamity	Nicola	3/12 stars
9	Hell-0-phone	David	9/12 stars
10	Pluck 'n' Roll	Brian and George	8/11 stars
11	Car-nage	Martina	10/10 stars

12	Dread Over Heels	Joe, Nicola and Simon	8/9 stars
13	Last Chance Saloon	Brian and Timmy	Brian wins
14	Last Gasp	Simon	6/7 stars
15	The Tower of Terror	Joe	6/6 stars
16	Wash 'n' Cry	Martina	2/5 stars
17	Celebrity Cyclone	David, George, Joe and Martina	4/4 stars
18	Danger Down Under	Joe	5/5 stars
19	Bushtucker Bonanza	George	4/5 stars
20	Fill Your Face	Martina	5/5 stars

WHAT TO FIND

Can you track down Keith and all the stars, our winner Joe, a green Mini, the mascara Nicola refused to give up and an ice cream topped with a critter?

I Scream cone

10 stars

Nicola's precious mascara

Joe winning

Keith

Australian Job Mini

2009

WINNER **Gino D'Acampo**

RUNNER UP **Kim Woodburn**

3rd Jimmy White 4th Justin Ryan 5th Stuart Manning
6th Sabrina Washington 7th George Hamilton 8th Joe Bugner
9th Samantha Fox 10th Colin McAllister
11th Lucy Benjamin 12th Katie Price
13th Camilla Dallerup

In true *I'm A Celebrity* style, Series 9 saw plenty of laughs as well as some serious bust-ups. Former boxer Joe Bugner once went toe to toe with Muhammad Ali, but nothing could have prepared him for the force of nature that is Kim Woodburn. She took an instant dislike to Joe and gave him some verbal uppercuts that left the old pro looking like he'd gone 10 rounds with, well, Muhammad Ali.

The truth is Kim Woodburn only had eyes for one man, the Hollywood superstar and ladies' favourite George Hamilton. Despite his advancing years, gorgeous George absolutely cruised through the jungle experience, regaling the camp with incredible tales of his glamorous Hollywood life and giving the boys some invaluable tips on wooing a lady.

The Hollywood heartthrob and the cleaning expert became an unlikely jungle couple, even if Kim's incredible snoring made it almost impossible for George to get his beauty sleep.

George and Kim weren't the only ones flirting, however – there was a bit of a jungle romance as well between actor Stuart Manning and Mis-Teeq singer Sabrina Washington.

Series 9 was also the first time a celebrity made a repeat visit to the Australian rainforest as a full-time resident, with the return of Katie Price, who first appeared on the show in 2004. Although, after being voted to do six Bushtucker Trials in a row, Katie decided to throw in the towel early... but not before she and Kim had taken part in one of the most stomach-churning eating trials in the history of the series.

All suited up, Gino D'Acampo and Stuart Manning make their way through the Slip 'n' Slide.

Every time Sabrina Washington touches the wire with her bee hat, Stuart is doused in gunk and critters.

Today's special in Chef Gino's kitchen: a live water spider.

The shining star of Series 9 was the irrepressible Gino D'Acampo. It seemed like nothing could wipe the smile off that man's face, and boy did the show's producers try. The Italian chef smiled his way through trials, ticks and more, showing off his impressive culinary skills in the process. In the end it was no surprise to see Gino walking away with the coveted jungle crown.

KEY MOMENTS

The celebrities drawing lots on a yacht ▮ Gino and Sam in All Washed Up ▮ Kim raging at Joe and flirting with George ▮ Sabrina in a bee suit ▮ Katie making a return, doing six trials in a row and then leaving again ▮ Gino and Stuart crawling through Slip 'n' Slide ▮ Gino winning the crown

WHAT TO FIND

Can you see Justin dressed up as a gingerbread man, Gino in a turkey suit and winning the show, a key to the Jungle Jail, the stars and Keith?

10 stars

Gino as a turkey

Gino as the King of the Jungle

Keith

Jail key

Justin as a gingerbread man

LIST OF TRIALS

1	All Washed Up	Gino and Sam	9/11 stars
2	Dreaded Descent	Kim	11/11 stars
3	Deathly Burrows	Katie	4/12 stars
4	Celebrity in a Bottle	Katie	6/12 stars
5	Jungle School	Katie	9/12 stars
6	Hell Holes Extreme	Katie	9/12 stars
7	Vile Vending	Katie and Kim	3/5 and 5/5 stars
8	Car-lamity!	Katie	11/12 stars
9	Bad Pit	Joe and Kim	9/11 stars
10	Slip 'n' Slide	Gino and Stuart	10/10 stars
11	Jungle Arms	Joe and Kim	10/10 stars
12	Scareway to Hell	Jimmy	5/9 stars
13	Great Barrier Grief	Justin	8/8 stars
14	Jungle Jail	Joe and Stuart	Stuart wins
15	Buzz Off	Sabrina and Stuart	3/7 stars
16	Memory Misery	Jimmy and Sabrina	1/6 stars
17	Off Your Trolley	Gino and Justin	3/5 stars
18	Hell Hill	Gino, Justin and Jimmy	4/4 stars
19	John Travolting	Kim	5/5 stars
20	Bushtucker Bonanza	Gino	5/5 stars
21	Flash Flood	Jimmy	4/5 stars

WINNER Stacey Solomon

RUNNER UP Shaun Ryder

3rd Jenny Eclair 4th Dom Joly 5th Kayla Collins
6th Aggro Santos 7th Linford Christie
8th Gillian McKeith 9th Britt Ekland
10th Alison Hammond 11th Lembit Öpik
12th Sheryl Gascoigne 13th Nigel Havers

Stacey Solomon and Dom Joly receive their undercover mission orders.

Laughing off imprisonment, hunger and angry snakes, jungle legend Shaun Ryder.

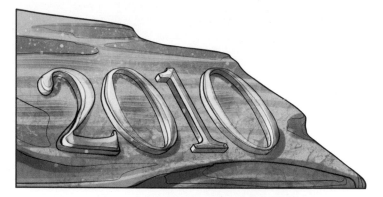

Series 10 of *I'm A Celebrity – Get Me Out Of Here!* featured a man who became many viewers' favourite-ever camper – Happy Mondays singer and genuine living legend Shaun Ryder. Shaun was funny, up for it and utterly fearless.

The absolute highlight of Shaun's time in the jungle came during an overnight challenge. While he was locked in a cell, Shaun's hand was in a box inhabited by one very bad-tempered snake. The snake sunk its fangs into Shaun's hand and would not let go. For many people this would have been a perfect moment to exit the challenge, or indeed the jungle. But not Shaun. Bleeding from his finger, he simply carried on, although he did utter a few choice words to the snake. They breed them tough in Manchester. Tougher than they breed them in the world of drama anyway, based on the evidence of actor Nigel Havers' short-lived appearance in an Immunity Challenge. The producers explained to Nigel that in this particular challenge, Jungle Justice, the slowest celebrities would receive an electric shock. Nigel's parting words were simple: 'I don't do electric shocks.' And he walked off the show forever.

But Nigel's refusal was thoroughly put in the shade by one of the weirdest, and most unforgettable, moments the programme has ever seen. From the start, health guru Gillian McKeith had struggled with life in the jungle. Then the evil public started doing what they always do when they smell fear: they sent her to do every single Bushtucker Trial they could.

Matters came to a head in a now-infamous trial when Gillian actually fainted live on national television. It was a truly jaw-dropping moment. In the end, Olympic champion

Linford Christie stepped up to the plate and took on the trial, but nobody ever remembers that. All we will ever recall is the sight of Medic Bob legging it over to help poor old Gillian.

One of the comedy highlights of the series was watching comedian Dom Joly and *X Factor* star Stacey Solomon going undercover in camp. No one will ever forget the moment Dom's fellow secret agent attempted to wake him up by throwing an unnecessarily large pebble at his head as he slept in his hammock. Pure comedy gold.

In the end Stacey, the camp's dottiest member, became the well-deserved Queen of the Jungle.

Stacey Solomon charmed the nation and was crowned Queen.

KEY MOMENTS

Shaun getting bitten by a snake ❦ Nigel complaining about electric shocks and walking off the show ❦ Gillian fainting live on television ❦ Dom and Stacey going undercover ❦ Stacey treading carefully in The Australian Job ❦ The trials kicking off with Hell Holes Kitchen ❦ Stacey winning

LIST OF TRIALS

1	Terrorvision (five parts)	Lembit and Kayla, Shaun and Gillian, Nigel and Sheryl, Aggro and Stacey, Linford and Britt	Lembit, Shaun, Sheryl, Stacey and Britt win
2	Crate Escape	Gillian and Lembit	Lembit wins
3	School Dinners	Gillian and Shaun	1/5 and 5/5 stars
4	The Australian Job	Stacey	4/10 stars
5	Aquatic Strife!	Gillian	4/12 stars
6	Calamity Cave	Gillian	5/13 stars
7	Dreaded Digger	Gillian	0/13 stars
8	Unfairground	Linford	12/13 stars
9	Fisherman's Fiend	Dom and Gillian	6/6 stars and 5/6 stars
10	Super Scario	Stacey and Aggro	12/12 stars
11	Starbugs	Alison and Jenny	8/12 stars
12	Creepy Crawly	Aggro	3/10 stars
13	The Dentalist	Alison and Kayla	Kayla wins
14	Dreaded Digger	Jenny	7/8 stars
15	Savage Garden Centre	Dom	3/7 stars
16	Stars in their Pies	Stacey	3/6 stars
17	Celebrity Cyclone	Dom, Jenny, Kayla, Shaun and Stacey	5/5 stars
18	Rank Banquet	Jenny, Shaun and Stacey	2/3, 3/3 and 3/3 stars
19	The Bush Spa	Stacey and Shaun	6/6 stars
20	Bush Spa	Shaun and Stacey	3/3 and 3/3 stars

WHAT TO FIND

Can you locate the human cockroach, the undercover mission tape recorder, Keith, the stars and Gillian's contraband?

Dom in a cockroach outfit

Mission tape recorder

Gillian's miso soup

Keith

Gillian's herb mix

Gillian's nettle tea bags

10 stars

2011

WINNER Dougie Poynter
RUNNER UP Mark Wright

3rd Fatima Whitbread 4th Antony Cotton 5th Willie Carson
6th Crissy Rock 7th Emily Scott 8th Jessica-Jane Clement
9th Lorraine Chase 10th Pat Sharp 11th Sinitta
12th Stefanie Powers 13th Freddie Starr

Series 11 of *I'm A Celebrity – Get Me Out Of Here!* got off to a dramatic start – but not in a good way. Freddie Starr had just put in a truly spectacular performance in a truly disgusting eating trial called The Greasy Spoon when he took ill and had to leave the show. *The Only Way is Essex* star Mark Wright, who faced Freddie across the table in that trial, probably wished the comedy legend had left before they'd both had to tuck into some absolutely revolting jungle titbits.

That wasn't the only moment of high drama early on this series. Liverpudlian comedian Crissy Rock incredibly lost her false teeth. She'd left them behind in a car before taking part in a skydive and the car had then driven off to its next destination. Luckily Crissy and her gnashers were later reunited.

Series 11 saw what is easily one of the most toe-curling moments in the history of the show. Javelin legend Fatima Whitbread was taking part in a very nasty trial – Fill Your Face Extreme – when she took the title perhaps a bit too literally. A cockroach sneaked up Fatima's nose and got itself stuck. Medic Bob was quickly on the scene, but watching Fatima struggle to get the little critter out had the nation hiding behind their cushions. Trooper that she is, Fatima shrugged off the experience and just carried on with her day.

The same can't be said for Sinitta. The singer struggled through three trials, winning four stars in Cable Cartastrophe and just two in Hell-evator before redeeming herself somewhat in Horrods. Nobody who heard her

Not even the critter crawling up into her nostril could stop Fatima Whitbread from winning the task.

blood-curdling screams will ever forget them. They were scarier than the trials.

But one camper stood head and shoulders above the rest in Series 11. As the bass player with boyband McFly, Dougie Poynter was already a favourite with younger ladies, but his performance in *I'm A Celebrity* brought him to a whole new audience. Of course, nobody loved Dougie more than *Coronation Street* star Antony Cotton – Antony absolutely adored his jungle pal, hugging the life out of him at every opportunity.

Having already played king in the celebrity royal court, it was only a matter of time before Dougie got to wear the crown for real.

The yabby was almost as unhappy about this trial as Sinitta.

Mark Wright faces up to a vile dish in the jungle's Greasy Spoon.

KEY MOMENTS

Freddie being forced to leave the show after The Greasy Spoon ⚡ Crissy leaving her teeth behind ⚡ Fatima blowing a cockroach out of her nose ⚡ Sinitta screaming through three trials ⚡ Antony and Dougie's friendship ⚡ The celebrity royal court ⚡ Celebrities scrambling around the maze in Rat Run ⚡ Mark and Antony identifying a cage of gorillas ⚡ Dougie winning

LIST OF TRIALS

#	Trial	Contestants	Result
1	Scales of Justice	Everyone except Emily, Pat and Sinitta	Antony, Crissy, Fatima, Lorraine and Mark win
2	The Greasy Spoon	Mark and Freddie	Freddie wins
3	Creepy Crypt	Mark and Stefanie	Mark wins
4	Rat Run	Dougie and Fatima	Fatima wins
5	Cable Car-tastrophe	Sinitta	4/11 stars
6	Crude Awakenings	Antony	8/12 stars
7	Hell-evator	Sinitta	2/12 stars
8	Horrods	Sinitta	5/12 stars
9	Head Trip	Pat	11/12 stars
10	Bushman's Bungalow	Pat	8/12 stars
11	Coral Grief	Emily	11/11 stars
12	Fair Dunk 'Um	Jessica-Jane	6/10 stars
13	Fill Your Face Extreme	Fatima and Pat	Fatima wins
14	Pits of Peril	Mark	8/8 stars
15	Mystery Box	Crissy and Willie	5/7 stars
16	Race Around the Clock	Dougie	6/6 stars
17	Splash and Grab	Antony and Fatima	2/5 stars
18	Celebrity Cyclone	Antony, Dougie, Fatima and Mark	4/4 stars
19	The Final Party	Dougie and Mark	4/4 and 4/4 stars

WHAT TO FIND

Can you locate Mark in a kangaroo suit, two kinds of headgear, a celeb stuck in the stocks, Keith and the stars?

Jester's hat from the medieval court

10 stars

Keith

Mark as a boxing kangaroo

Mark's bandana

A celeb in the stocks

WINNER Charlie Brooks

RUNNER UP Ashley Roberts

3rd David Haye 4th Eric Bristow 5th Hugo Taylor
6th Rosemary Shrager 7th Helen Flanagan
8th Colin Baker 9th Linda Robson
10th Limahl 11th Nadine Dorries
12th Brian Conley

Charlie Brooks and Ashley Roberts raise a bottle at their final dinner in the camp.

Eric Bristow is not impressed with Rosemary Shrager's plans to cook an ostrich egg omelette.

There was drama before Series 12 of *I'm a Celebrity* even got started, as Conservative MP Nadine Dorries found herself suspended by the party, who weren't best pleased about an honourable member entering the jungle.

But when it came to rejections, nobody comes close to Helen Flanagan. The *Coronation Street* actress made jungle history with her relentless rejections of trial after trial. In Cruelty Towers, Helen won a grand total of zero stars, and she repeated that feat in Come Dive With Me and Rodent Run. Eventually Kajagoogoo singer Limahl couldn't help but point out that she should have read the small print before joining the show... which went down well.

On the plus side, former *Dr Who* Colin Baker shifted a few pounds due to a serious lack of grub, so he was pretty pleased. And on the subject of food, late arrival Rosemary Shrager definitely made an impact. The chef got right up the nose of darts legend Eric Bristow, with her bossiness and snarky comments, particularly around dinner time. Maybe it was lucky that, thanks to Helen, there was rarely much food in the first place.

The lack of food seemed to hit *Made In Chelsea* star Hugo Taylor the worst – in the end he was little more than skin, bones and a bad temper.

Eric Bristow was one of the stars of the series, not that anyone knew what he was saying half the time. Let's just say he was a bit of a mumbler. Mind you, having watched Eric rap with Colin, maybe that was for the best.

The only people who just about managed to maintain their sense of humour were *EastEnders* star Charlie Brooks and Pussycat Doll Ashley Roberts. They were the last celebrities standing, with Charlie claiming the crown.

Helen Flanagan comes under attack from a swarm of flies.

The unlikeliest rap duo of the year, Colin Baker and Eric Bristow.

WHAT TO FIND

Apart from Keith and the stars, can you see Charlie celebrating her victory, a dartboard, a pair of boxing gloves and Ashley as a gnome in a red bikini?

David's boxing gloves

10 stars

Keith

Charlie as Queen of the Jungle

Ashley as a garden gnome

Dartboard from Jungle Darts

KEY MOMENTS

The celebrities splitting into two camps to compete for a luxury night ⭐ Helen winning a grand total of 0 stars in three trials ⭐ Hugo facing a sewer of creatures in Savage Sewer ⭐ Rosemary and Eric bickering ⭐ Eric and Colin's rap ⭐ All the celebrities facing a glass coffin in Bed Bugs ⭐ Charlie claiming the crown

LIST OF TRIALS

1	Special Delivery	David and Hugo	David wins
2	Bug Burial	Helen and Nadine	Both quit
3	Rotten Rhymes	Helen and Nadine	Nadine wins
4	Cruelty Towers	Helen	0/10 stars
5	Come Dive with Me	Helen and Charlie	0/6 and 3/6 stars
6	Rodent Run	Helen	0/12 stars
7	Deadly Delivery	Helen	12/12 stars
8	Bad Day at the Office	Helen	5/12 stars
9	Savage Sewer	Hugo	9/11 stars
10	Terror Train	Ashley	8/10 stars

11	Scare Plane	David	9/9 stars
12	Drown and Out	Hugo	8/8 stars
13	The Panic Rooms	Colin and Charlie, Eric and Rosemary	4/4 and 1/4 stars
14	Cruelty Towers	David	6/7 stars
15	The Great Escape	Eric	5/6 stars
16	Jungle Walk of Shame	Ashley and Charlie	4/5 stars
17	Celebrity Cyclone	Ashley, Charlie, David and Eric	4/4 stars
18	Well of Hell	David	3/3 stars
19	Final Feast	Ashley and Charlie	4/4 and 4/4 stars

2013

WINNER Kian Egan

RUNNER UP David Emanuel

3rd Lucy Pargeter 4th Joey Essex 5th Amy Willerton
6th Rebecca Adlington 7th Alfonso Ribeiro
8th Steve Davis 9th Matthew Wright
10th Vincent Simone 11th Laila Morse
12th Annabel Giles

Series 13 of *I'm A Celebrity* had many memorable moments, but surely the biggest star to come out of the jungle that year was the fantastic Joey Essex. In just three weeks, Joey achieved so many things: he made loads of new friends, he reinvented the English language and, above all, he learnt how to tell the time. Millions of viewers fell in love with Joey and, for many of them, it was a real shock when he wasn't crowned King of the Jungle.

It wasn't all a big love in. *EastEnders* actress Laila Morse definitely wasn't in love with one camper in particular, model Amy Willerton, and used some very tasty language to make her point.

Amy also found herself at the centre of one of the biggest stories of the series when she became embroiled in the contraband scandal. It turned out that Amy had smuggled a load of luxuries into camp, including that basic survival essential – chewing gum. And it seemed like it wasn't so much the fact that Amy had smuggled stuff in that got up some people's noses, as the fact that she hadn't shared her goodies with them.

In the end, Amy handed back the contraband to stop the camp being penalised, but as far as Laila was concerned, the damage was done.

Talking of dramatic stories, Olympic Gold medallist, swimmer Rebecca Adlington stunned the camp with her shock revelation to Joey Essex that when she was in training she regularly peed in the pool rather than climb out to go to the loo. Poor old Joey looked genuinely appalled.

When the world heard that Alfonso Ribeiro was booked on the show, we were all waiting with bated breath for him to deliver his classic *Fresh Prince of Bel Air* dance moves. In the end it took over a week, but it was well worth the wait when they finally arrived.

What we didn't expect to see was the normally very calm Alfonso blowing his top at *The Wright Stuff* presenter Matthew Wright. But then, Matthew was kind of annoying. Bizarrely enough, matters came to a head during a discussion about contracts. A very showbiz fallout.

For the single funniest moment in Series 13, look no further than snooker legend Steve Davis. Steve's fellow campers sent him to take on a trial called Scares Rock. And while he was making his way around the trial, he suddenly tripped, plunged off Scares Rock and fell into the pool. It took Ant and Dec an age to compose themselves.

Alfonso Ribeiro finally shows his *Fresh Prince of Bel Air* moves.

Not for the first time, a boyband singer looked nailed on to win the crown from the moment he entered the jungle, and that was how things turned out with former Westlife singer Kian Egan. Of course, it didn't hurt that Kian shed floods of tears during a Halfway Holiday Treat when he was reunited with his wife. You could almost hear the people of Britain grabbing their phones to vote for him. The runner up was Princess Diana's dress designer, the incredibly charming and well-behaved David Emanuel.

Joey Essex provided plenty of moments of I'm a Celebrity gold.

KEY MOMENTS

Joey's journey ⚡ Amy sneaks luxuries into the camp ⚡ Vincent's tighty whities ⚡ Alfonso dancing ⚡ Alfonso and Matthew fall out over contracts ⚡ Vincent in a spider costume ⚡ Steve falls off Scares Rock ⚡ Kian weeps during a Halfway Holiday Treat ⚡ Kian wins

LIST OF TRIALS

#	Trial	Contestants	Result
1	Turntable of Terror	Laila and David, Amy and Matthew, Rebecca and Kian, Steve and Alfonso, Joey and Lucy	winners: David, Matthew, Kian, Alfonso, Lucy
2	Monday Night Takeaway	Matthew and Joey	Joey wins
3	Up to Your Neck in It	Matthew and Joey	Joey wins
4	Sub-merged	Joey	7/10 stars
5	Hang Glider from Hell	Amy	7/10 stars
6	Critter Canteen	Annabel and Vincent	Vincent wins
7	Cavern of Claws	Joey	8/12 stars
8	Critters Got Talent	Joey	10/12 stars
9	In Cave Danger	Kian	9/9 stars
10	Limo Scream	Lucy	10/12 stars
11	Drown Under	Rebecca	10/10 stars
12	As Scream on TV	David	8/9 stars
13	Critter Crates	Alfonso, Amy, Annabel, Joey, Kian, Lucy, Matthew, Steve	Matthew wins
14	Who Dares Wins Stars	Laila	10/11 stars
15	Scares Rock	Steve	3/10 stars
16	Plank of Peril	Alfonso and Kian	8/8 stars
17	Surf and Turf	Amy	6/7 stars
18	Celebrity Cyclone	Amy, David, Joey, Kian, Lucy	5/5 stars
19	In a Spin	David, Kian and Lucy	2/3 stars
20	Final Feast	David and Kian	4/4 and 4/4 stars

WHAT TO FIND

Of course we need to hide Matthew in a bikini... can you find him? Also lurking in the jungle are a koala in shades, Keith, the stars and a praying mantis, a frog and a gecko from the cut scenes.

Matthew in a white bikini

Koala in shades

Keith

10 stars

Silhouette of a gecko

Bulging-eyed frog

Praying mantis

WINNER Carl 'Foggy' Fogarty

RUNNER UP Jake Quickenden

3rd Melanie Sykes 4th Edwina Currie
5th Tinchy Stryder 6th Kendra Wilkinson
7th Vicki Michelle 8th Michael Buerk
9th Nadia Forde 10th Jimmy Bullard
11th Craig Charles 12th Gemma Collins

Edwina Currie conducted a blazing row with Kendra Wilkinson from the comfort of her bed.

Game for pretty much anything, Michael Buerk took to the tightrope in full parrot finery.

Series 14 of *I'm a Celebrity – Get Me Out Of Here!* saw one of the most impressive and surprising casts ever to move into the nation's favourite jungle. From World Champion motorcyclists to legendary newsreaders and seasoned politicians, this series had them all.

Jimmy Bullard enjoyed his 'bants' and, at first, we all loved his cheeky chat. But viewers felt Jimmy pushed it too far with *X Factor* finalist Jake Quickenden and gave the former footballer an early bath – Jimmy was the first to be voted out of camp. Up until that point, Jimmy and former superbike champ Carl 'Foggy' Fogarty had been enjoying a proper bromance. But Foggy was more than happy to buddy up with Jake after Jimmy got his marching orders.

Two other celebrities took their leave early: *Red Dwarf* star Craig Charles had to exit for personal reasons and *TOWIE* star Gemma Collins had to go because... well, there wasn't really a good reason, she just didn't fancy it.

Unlike Gemma, some people did enjoy camp life, none more so than veteran newsreader Michael Buerk. Michael dressed up as a parrot for a challenge, ran a jungle office with presenter Melanie Sykes and, most memorably of all, performed a rap with musician Tinchy Stryder. It doesn't get better than that. He'd probably never seen the show in his life, but Michael proved he was a good sport.

Former politician Edwina Currie also had a great time, doing what she enjoys best – arguing. She had a bust-up with Melanie about whether or not men need women and a series of flare-ups with Playboy Bunny and reality star Kendra Wilkinson about whether people should live their lives for themselves or other people. To her credit, Kendra stood her ground with Edwina, while Edwina barely got out of her hammock. Edwina also starred in one memorable scene where, sitting entirely on her own, she dished out insults to her least favourite campers.

The most shocking – and hilarious – trial moment of Series 14 featured Foggy. Along with Jimmy, Melanie and Tinchy, he took a trip to the Vile Vineyard for a drinking trial. And no one who saw it will ever forget the sight of Foggy wearing a gory bloodstained moustache after one particularly unpleasant cocktail.

If only for that moment, Foggy fully deserved to claim the jungle crown, with the lovable Jake as his runner-up.

Unfortunately for 'Foggy' Fogarty, that's not tomato juice.

KEY MOMENTS

Celebrities entering the camp on a zip wire ⚡ Craig and Gemma leaving in the first few days ⚡ Michael and Tinchy rapping ⚡ Edwina badmouthing other celebrities all on her own ⚡ Foggy avoiding a giant boulder in Tunnels of Terror ⚡ Foggy's blood moustache ⚡ The celebs being entombed in a Mayan temple in the final Immunity challenge ⚡ Foggy winning

LIST OF TRIALS

#	Trial	Celebrity	Stars
1	Snakes in a Drain	Foggy	6/6 stars
2	Tunnel of Terror	Jimmy	4/6 stars
3	Chamber of Horrors	Tinchy	4/7 stars
4	Bush Bunker	Craig and Nadia	7/10 stars
5	Terror Tavern	Jimmy and Kendra	10/10 stars
6	Cockroach Shaker	Kendra	1/10 stars
7	The Catacombs of Doom	Kendra	2/10 stars
8	Hell's Kitchen	Melanie	9/10 stars
9	The Critter Cube	Jake	10/10 stars
10	The Critter Cube	Jimmy	1/1 star
11	Grim Gallery	Kendra	1/10 stars
12	The Shed of Dread	Jimmy and Foggy	10/10 stars
13	Little House on the Scary	Kendra	10/10 stars
14	Pipes of Peril	Edwina and Kendra	6/10 stars
15	Cabin Fever	Edwina	8/10 stars
16	Down the Chain	Foggy and Jake	Jake wins
17	Vile Vineyard	Foggy, Jimmy, Melanie and Tinchy	10/10 stars
18	The Deadly Dunker	Michael and Vicki	7/9 stars
19	Boulder Dash	Foggy	8/8 stars
20	The Catacombs of Doom	Tinchy	6/7 stars
21	Critter Conveyor	Kendra and Melanie	6/6 stars
22	Celebrity Cyclone	Edwina, Foggy, Jake and Melanie	4/4 stars
23	Fill Your Face	Jake	5/5 stars
24	Bushtucker Bonanza	Foggy	5/5 stars
25	Drown and Out	Melanie	5/5 stars

WHAT TO FIND

Can you find Kendra in a cocktail shaker full of critters, a parrot wearing shades, a tape recorder, a bag of swag, Keith and all the stars?

Tape recorder with CIA mission on it

10 stars

Keith

Kendra in the cocktail shaker

Macaw in sunglasses

Bag of Dingo Dollars

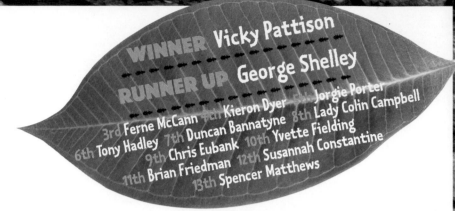

Series 15 of *I'm A Celebrity – Get Me Out Of Here!* was quite simply one of the most explosive, crazy and wonderful pieces of television you will ever see. And one of the main reasons for this was the presence of actual (okay, possible) royalty, Lady Colin Campbell.

You can say what you want about Lady C (and *Dragon's Den* star Duncan Bannatyne and Spandau Ballet singer Tony Hadley most definitely did) but that lady is a genuine character.

She had an ongoing feud with Tony. They fought after he pulled her up for throwing a beetle on the fire. She called him a pretentious piffler – and worse. They squabbled after Lady C bought a can of tomato soup from the jungle vending machine, after which she described him as a buffoon.

Lady C's outbursts weren't limited to the camp. She also managed to cause strife at the Bushtucker Trial clearing, when she refused to take on the Panic Pit trial.

She even refused to take part in a washing-up challenge with *Most Haunted* presenter Yvette Fielding, leaving Yvette speechless – and she's had to deal with actual ghosts. In short, Lady C wound the entire camp up from start to finish, but while many of the celebrities simply couldn't stand the sight of her, the Lady had the viewing nation hooked.

There was plenty more to enjoy in Series 15. Who can forget Chris Eubank's classic backwards walk, displayed to perfection during a Dingo Dollar Challenge? Ant's impersonation of the former boxer was one of the highlights of the show that year.

Unleashing hitherto unexpected powers of persuasion, Chris Eubank talked Kieron Dyer into staying.

Chris showed his softer side when he persuaded footballer Kieron Dyer not to walk off the show. Kieron had behaved like a true gent, defending Lady C again and again in camp, but even he finally snapped and if it hadn't been for Chris's words, he would have been heading for an early bath.

While the other campmates were proving to be mad, bad and occasionally downright weird, *Geordie Shore* star Vicky Pattison was just plain lovable. She and fellow reality TV star Ferne McCann might have been late arrivals, but once they'd got over some early friction with choreographer Brian Friedman, Vicky proved to be a formidable presence in camp. In total, Vicky took on a whopping seven trials as she cruised towards the final day and a well-deserved victory.

Vicky Pattinson took to the jungle like a flying squirrel to an acorn.

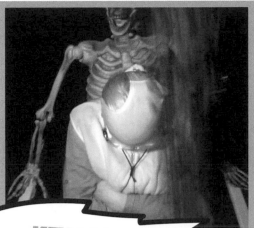

Yvette Fielding felt right at home in the Jungle Ghost Train.

KEY MOMENTS

Lady Colin Campbell winding everyone up ❧ Chris's backwards walk ❧ Celebrities getting the ride of their lives in Jungle Ghost Train ❧ Vicky taking on seven trials ❧ The celebs competing in teams in You Bad Buoys ❧ Vicky flying through the air in a squirrel costume ❧ The celebs getting covered in critters in Scare Fair ❧ Vicky taking the crown

WHAT TO FIND

Aside from Keith and the stars, can you spot Brian in a chicken suit, a dancing skeleton, a pair of emus and a DeLorean?

Skeleton wearing sunglasses

10 stars

DeLorean from Saturday Fright at the Movies

Two adorable emus

Keith

Brian dressed as a chicken

LIST OF TRIALS

1	Hell evated	Chris, George, Jorgie, Kieron, Lady C and Tony	10/10 stars
2	Disaster Chef	Jorgie and Lady C	10/10 stars
3	Panic Pit	Lady C	0/10 stars
4	Jungle Ghost Train	Brian, George, Jorgie, Kieron and Yvette	3/5 stars
5	Scare Fair	Chris, Duncan, Lady C, Susannah and Tony	3/5 stars
6	Dicing with Danger	Ferne, Spencer and Vicky	Ferne wins
7	Every Critter Counts	Brian, Jorgie and Lady C	Lady C wins
8	Cocktails and Screams	All celebrities	Chris, Duncan, Ferne, Kieron, Lady C, Tony and Vicky win
9	The Trailer of Torment	Brian, George, Jorgie, Susannah and Yvette	5/5 stars
10	Horri-flying Circus	Ferne and Vicky	6/12 stars
11	Helmets of Hell	Lady C	9/12 stars

12	Floods of Fear	Ferne	10/12 stars
13	The Critter Shop of Horrors	Brian	12/12 stars
14	Scarier 51	Lady C	0/12 stars
15	Steps to Hell	Kieron, Tony and Vicky	Kieron wins
16	Saturday Fright at the Movies	George	10/11 stars
17	Depths of Despair	Duncan and Tony	9/11 stars
18	Scarier 52	Kieron	9/10 stars
19	Badvent Calendar	Vicky	9/9 stars
20	Panic Pit Part 2	Ferne	8/8 stars
21	Horrible Heist	Jorgie and Kieron	3/7 stars
22	Twisted Tombola	Kieron and Vicky	5/6 stars
23	Celebrity Cyclone	Ferne, George, Jorgie, Kieron and Vicky	5/5 stars
24	Surf & Turf	Vicky	4/4 stars
25	Bushtucker Bonanza	Ferne	4/4 stars
26	Critter Attack	George	4/4 stars

2016

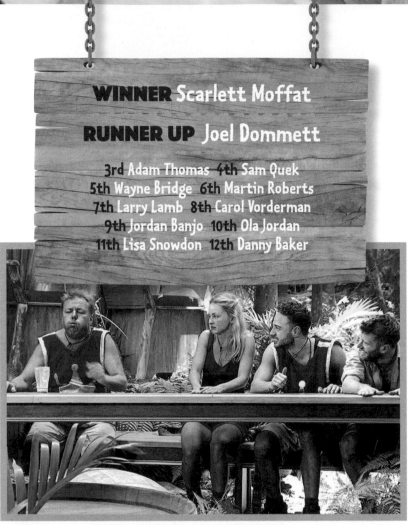

WINNER **Scarlett Moffat**

RUNNER UP **Joel Dommett**

3rd Adam Thomas 4th Sam Quek
5th Wayne Bridge 6th Martin Roberts
7th Larry Lamb 8th Carol Vorderman
9th Jordan Banjo 10th Ola Jordan
11th Lisa Snowdon 12th Danny Baker

Martin Roberts enjoys a pint in the Bush Brewery with Ola Jordan, Adam Thomas and Joel Dommett.

Scarlett Moffat's amazing arrray of facial expressions said it all during the Big Bush Bake Off.

Series 16 of *I'm A Celebrity – Get Me Out Of Here!* got off to an electric start when celebrities including comedian Joel Dommett and former *Countdown* presenter Carol Vorderman took on a truly terrifying challenge – walking the plank 96m (300 feet) up in the air. It made your legs turn to jelly just watching it.

This series had plenty of laughs, some great characters and not a lot of squabbling. The jungle also saw a bit of romance, although that was Ant's infatuation with *EastEnders* star and daddy of the camp, Larry Lamb. Larry was a father figure to dancer Jordan Banjo and Chelsea legend Wayne Bridge, who proved that footballers really can have a sensitive side.

One person Larry didn't love was *Homes Under the Hammer* presenter Martin Roberts, who suggested drawing straws to decide who would face the Panic Pipeline. In the end that was exactly how Wayne got the job, but Larry still gave Martin a major lecture about jungle protocol.

You could kind of see why Martin wound Larry up from his role in the Claim of Thrones challenge. Martin lost his royal status during one of the most incredible Bushtucker Trials ever, Claim of Thrones: The Bush Brewery, which saw him retching after downing a series of repulsive drinks. Rather than take the defeat with good grace, when he was later summoned to the royal camp, Martin pretended to trip and threw a bowl of water over *Emmerdale* star Adam Thomas. Very cheeky. After a good cry, Martin eventually changed his behaviour and the camp began to warm to him.

Adam later got his own back after a successful Dingo Dollar Challenge, when he denied Martin a delicious piece of chocolate – the very definition of sweet revenge.

Adam was the camp jester, although the smile was wiped off his face when, along with Joel, he came face to face with his greatest fear – spiders – in a Creepy Cabin overnight challenge. There were hundreds of the things and Adam's antics were absolutely hilarious.

Gogglebox regular Scarlett Moffatt made her name watching TV, but given a starring role in the jungle, she was absolutely fantastic and viewers adored her. From joining forces with Carol in the Big Bush Bake Off trial to loving every second in the legendary Celebrity Cyclone, Scarlett was the star of the series and fully deserved to win that precious crown of twigs.

Joel Dommett and Adam Thomas in the Celebrity Cyclone.

KEY MOMENTS

Celebrities walking the plank ⚬ Larrry's fatherly moments with Jordan and Wayne ⚬ Larry giving Martin a dressing down ⚬ Martin losing his royal status in Claim of Thrones: The Bush Brewery ⚬ Jungle creatures swarming floating celebrity heads in Fright at the Museum ⚬ The celebs getting covered in cockroaches in Vicious Circle ⚬ The best-ever Celebrity Cyclone ⚬ Scarlett winning

LIST OF TRIALS

#	Trial	Contestants	Result
1	Tomb of Torment	Jordan, Ola, Sam and Scarlett	10/10 stars
2	Big Bush Bake Off	Carol and Scarlett	9/10 stars
3	Stranded	Adam, Joel, Jordan and Wayne	4/10 stars
4	The Great Ascent	Joel	10/10 stars
5	The Hungry Games: Rank Tanks	Carol, Danny, Martin and Sam	Carol and Danny win
6	THG: Catch a Falling Critter	Adam, Joel, Jordan, Larry, Lisa, Martin, Sam and Scarlett	Adam, Jordan, Ola and Wayne win
7	THG: The Final	All celebrities	Adam, Carol, Danny, Jordan, Ola and Wayne
8	Rancid Retreat	Joel, Larry, Lisa, Martin, Sam and Scarlett	5/6 stars
9	Hell Hollow	Martin	8/12 stars
10	Bushtucker Food Factory	Adam	11/12 stars
11	Cage Rage	Adam and Danny	12/12 stars
12	Claim of Thrones: Vicious Circle	All celebrities	Adam, Martin, Sam and Wayne win
13	CoT: The Bush Brewery	Adam, Martin, Joel and Ola	Adam and Ola win
14	CoT: Gates to Hell	Adam, Wayne, Lisa and Scarlett	Adam and Wayne win
15	Panic Pipeline	Wayne	11/11 stars
16	Pick 'n' Critz	Adam and Martin	11/11 stars
17	Hot Scare Ballooning	Carol and Sam	10/10 stars
18	Hell or High Water	Jordan and Larry	9/9 stars
19	Wicked Windmill	Joel and Sam	3/8 stars
20	Critter Console	Scarlett	6/7 stars
21	Knickerbocker Gory	Adam	6/6 stars
22	Celebrity Cyclone	Adam, Joel, Sam and Scarlett	4/4 stars
23	Fill Your Face	Adam	5/5 stars
24	Bushtucker Bonanza	Joel	5/5 stars
25	Cavern of Claws	Scarlett	5/5 stars

WHAT TO FIND

Can you spot our winner Scarlett, Joel in a crab suit, Martin with a yabby in his mouth, a knight, the stars and Keith?

Martin with a yabby

Keith

10 stars

Joel dressed as a crab

Scarlett wins the crown

A knight of the jungle

LEAVING THE JUNGLE

We're almost out of time, so for the final part of our *I'm A Celebrity* story, we thought we'd take a look at an experience shared by every star, or at least all the ones who stick it out until the public decides to give them the boot: the jungle exit.

KEY MOMENTS

Nicola McLean's 'fond' farewell to David Van Day in 2008 ❧ Rodney Marsh greeting his sparring partner Lynne Franks ❧ Rosemary Shrager discovering she'd lost a staggering 2 stone 3 pounds during her jungle stay in 2012 ❧ Scarlett's chicken kebab detour in 2016

The moment Ant and Dec announce the name of the next camper to go, there's a whirlwind of activity. First we have the hurried goodbyes to fellow campmates – all of whom, the celeb now knows, are more popular than they are. This is a chance to offer warm words of encouragement and support to your fellow celebs, although in Series 8, model Nicola McLean used it as an opportunity to get in one last dig at her nemesis, David Van Day: 'Your game's worked, well done, but everyone watch out, because there's a snake in the grass.'

After saying goodbye to the others, the celebrity leaving the jungle grabs their rucksack and is escorted across a series of bridges and onto the studio floor for a chat with Ant and Dec. At the end of the interview, the boys utter the immortal words, 'You're a celebrity, get yourself out of here' and the celeb heads off over that final bridge while a load of fireworks go off.

The celeb's other half is usually waiting at the other end of the bridge, and there's a load of smooching and hugging in front of a pack of photographers. You really have to feel for the celeb's partner, who gets to be manhandled by a smelly, sweaty and tearful celeb live on national television. Then the show is over.

The celeb heads for a quick chat with the show's psychiatrist to make sure they still have all their marbles. Then they pop in for a check-up with Medic Bob, who lets them know how much weight they've lost during their time in the jungle. Then they head straight into the staff canteen next door to pile most of it back on again.

Traditionally, the next stop for departing celebs is the local McDonald's drive-thru, where our former campers shamelessly gorge themselves on the carbs and sugar they've been missing for the last few weeks. Series 16 winner Scarlett Moffatt had way too much class for that kind of behaviour and instructed her driver not to stop at the McDonald's under any circumstances. She insisted he take her to the local kebab shop instead.

Christopher Biggins walks over the bridge and out of the jungle as the winner in 2007.

Martin Roberts has a revelatory journey to the hotel in 2016.

Palazzo Versace
GOLD COAST AUSTRALIA

One of the world's top five-star luxury hotels, the Palazzo Versace, awaits our happy campers.

Sam Quek reaquaints herself with soft furnishings.

The last stop for our campers is the Hotel Palazzo Versace in Surfers Paradise. Here we witness the final *I'm A Celebrity* tradition: it's the moment our celeb comes face to face with a load of former campmates who've had a shower and a haircut and are no longer wearing their name on their shirt. The celeb's look of sheer bemusement says it all: 'I'm pretty sure I know you from somewhere – but I can't put a name to the face.'

When the confusion has been cleared up and more hugs and kisses have been shared, the celebrity finally retires to their bedroom. After that... well, that's not really any of our business, now is it?

You can leave your hat on – Wayne Bridge tucks in to a bathtime burger.

And that's where we leave you... Joel Dommett requests a bit of privacy for some well-needed ablutions, with cheesecake, naturally.

WHAT TO FIND

Aside from Keith and the stars, can you find the first King of the Jungle, Scarlett's victory meal, prize money, tabloid headlines and a happy rat?

10 stars

Scarlett's chicken kebab

Keith

EAC WINNER. OUT OF HERE!

Stack of newspapers

Dingo Dollars

Our first winner, Tony

A rat leaving the camp for his hols

ANSWERS

2002
pages 6–7

Fruit bat

Tony

Machete in tree

Chameleon's eye

Keith

2003
pages 10–11

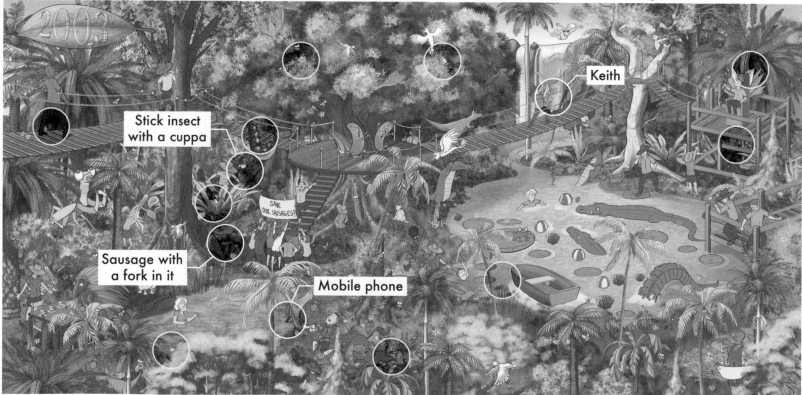

Keith

Stick insect
with a cuppa

Sausage with
a fork in it

Mobile phone

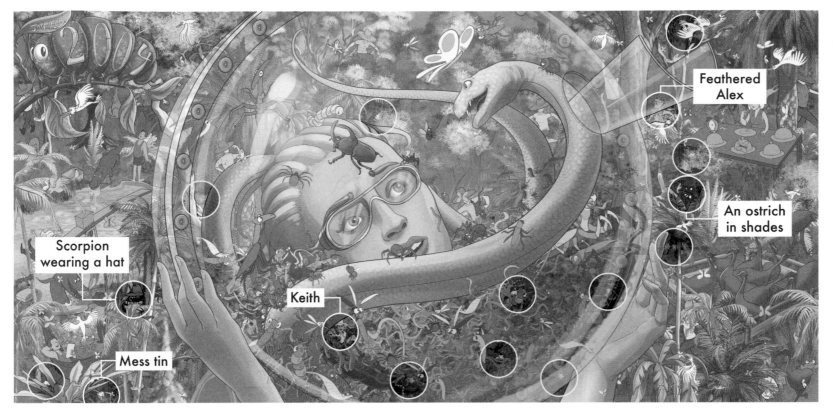

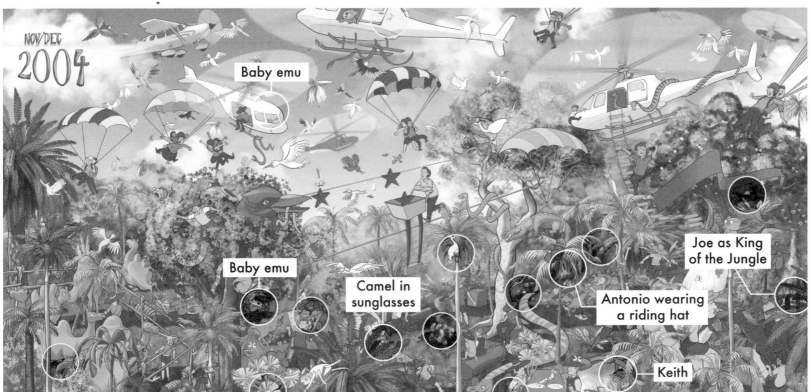

2004 (1)
pages 14–15

2004 (2)
pages 18–19

2005
pages 22–23

2006
pages 26–27

2009
pages 38–39

2010
pages 42–43

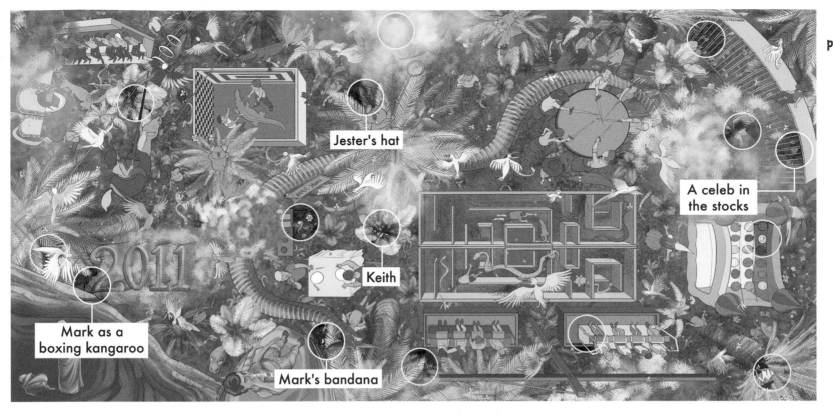

Jester's hat

A celeb in the stocks

Keith

Mark as a boxing kangaroo

Mark's bandana

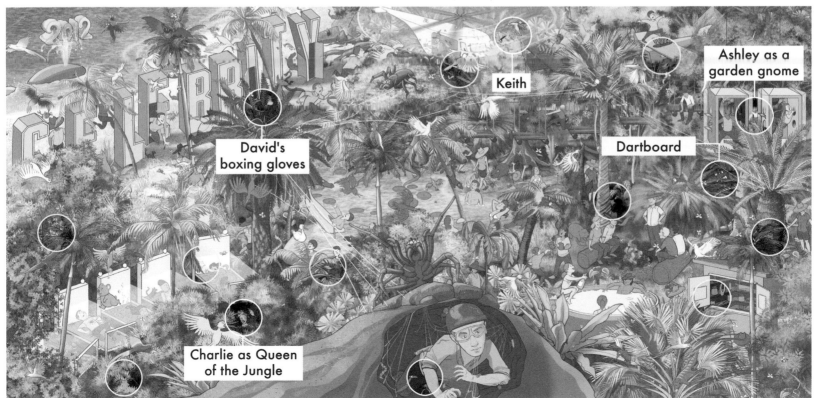

Keith

Ashley as a garden gnome

David's boxing gloves

Dartboard

Charlie as Queen of the Jungle

2013
pages 54–55

- Praying mantis
- Matthew in a white bikini
- Bulging-eyed frog
- Silhouette of a gecko
- Koala in shades
- Keith

2014
pages 58–59

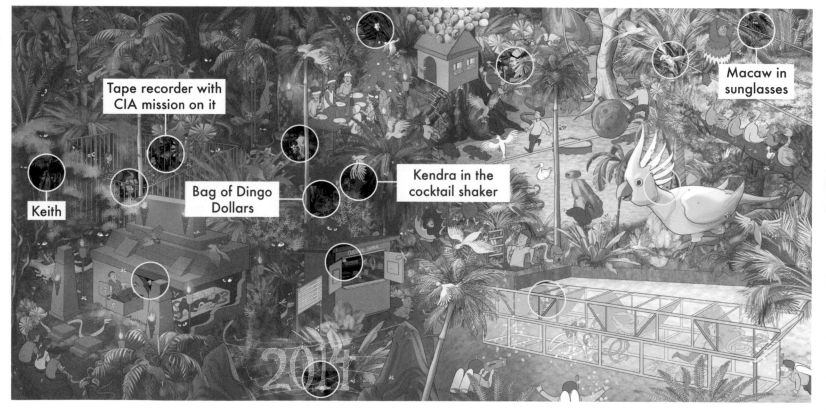

- Tape recorder with CIA mission on it
- Keith
- Bag of Dingo Dollars
- Kendra in the cocktail shaker
- Macaw in sunglasses

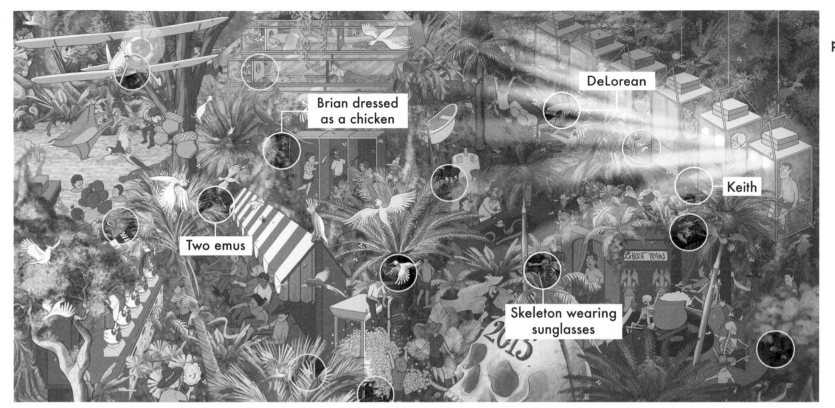

An Hachette UK Company
www.hachette.co.uk

First published in Great Britain in 2017 by Hamlyn, a division of Octopus Publishing Group Ltd
Carmelite House, 50 Victoria Embankment, London EC4Y 0DZ
www.octopusbooks.co.uk
www.octopusbooksusa.com

Distributed in the US by Hachette Book Group, 1290 Avenue of the Americas, 4th and 5th Floors, New York, NY 10104

Distributed in Canada by Canadian Manda Group, 664 Annette Street, Toronto, Ontario, Canada M6S 2C8

Mark Cowley asserts the moral right to be identified as the author of this work.

ISBN 978 0 60063 531 4

A CIP catalogue record for this book is available from the British Library.

Printed and bound in Italy

10 9 8 7 6 5 4 3 2 1

Picture acknowledgements
Photographs ©ITV/Rex/Shutterstock

Text by Mark Cowley
Illustrations by Bill Hope

Publishing Director Trevor Davies
Art Director Juliette Norsworthy
Senior Editor Alex Stetter
Editorial Assistant Mala Sanghera-Warren
Senior Production Manager Peter Hunt